THE MAD POTTER

GEORGE E. OHR
ECCENTRIC GENIUS

JAN GREENBERG
& SANDRA JORDAN

A NEAL PORTER BOOK
ROARING BROOK PRESS
NEW YORK

In memory of Judith Aronson, dear friend and mentor —J.G.
For Aunt Lindsay and Uncle David, let me count the ways —S.J.

ACKNOWLEDGMENTS

Putting a book together takes the thought and patient effort of many people who are kind enough to answer our questions and point us in the right direction. We are grateful.

Thank-you to Robert A. Ellison, Jr. and Rosaire Appel for sharing their insights about George Ohr, as well as their amazing collection of works by Ohr, many of which appear in the pages of this book; to Eugene and Carolyn Hecht, whose encyclopedic knowledge of Ohr's life and work greatly enhanced our understanding of The Mad Potter. Both Ellison and the Hechts graciously read our manuscript and offered advice. Their books and essays about George Ohr also gave us invaluable information and inspiration.

Thanks go to Edward R. and Ann Hudson for their introduction to Bob Ellison and for their many years of friendship; to Hugh Grant, founding director and curator of the Kirkland Museum of Fine and Decorative Art in Denver; as well as Christopher Herron and Maya D. Wright, for their tour of the museum and for the pieces by Ohr that are reproduced here; and to David Charak for the delightful teapot in his collection, which sports Ohr's original clay pricetag.

Our heartfelt thanks to Denny Mecham, the director of the Ohr-O'Keefe Museum in Biloxi, for providing key information about the museum; to Barbara Ross, head curator of the museum, who shared all the museum's resources, even during the 2012 storm that battered the Gulf Coast, and cheerfully responded to our many queries over the months that we worked on this book; and to Julie Gustafson, who gave us a spirited hardhat tour of the museum buildings designed by Frank Gehry.

Thanks go to Dennis Scholl, whose Emmy-winning documentary Dancing with the Trees *both informed and inspired us. Gratitude to Win Glasgow who gave a close-up, firsthand tutorial in working clay on the wheel. Kristi Finefield at the Library of Congress made complicated technical mysteries look easy. Thanks go to Alice Cooney Frelinghuysen, curator of decorative arts at the Metropolitan Museum, for her prompt attention to our requests. We could not have done without the generous support of computer savvy Courtney Meyer and photographer Mike Martin, both of Greenberg Gallery. We appreciate the continued guidance of our agent, George Nicholson. As always, special thanks go to our esteemed editor, Neal Porter, and valued designer, Jennifer Browne, who encourage, support, and do their talented best to make us look good. A grateful nod to the Roaring Brook team: managing editor, Jill Freshney, who smoothes the path of books that come into her hands; Susan Doran, who makes tricky production problems melt away; Lucy del Priore, who daily performs amazing feats of promotion and publicity; and Emily Feinberg, who capably assisted in the completion of this project.*

A Neal Porter Book
Published by Roaring Brook Press
Roaring Brook Press is a division of Holtzbrinck Publishing Holdings Limited Partnership
175 Fifth Avenue, New York, New York 10010
mackids.com

Library of Congress Cataloging-in-Publication Data
Greenberg, Jan, 1942–
    The mad potter : George E. Ohr, eccentric genius / Jan Greenberg and
Sandra Jordan. — First edition.
      pages cm
    "A Neal Porter Book."
    Includes bibliographical references and index.
    ISBN 978-1-59643-810-1 (hardcover : alk. paper)
1. Ohr, George E., 1857–1918—Juvenile literature. 2. Potters—United
States—Biography—Juvenile literature. 3. Art pottery, American—
Mississippi—Biloxi—Juvenile literature. I. Jordan, Sandra
(Sandra Jane Fairfax) II. Title.
    NK4210.O42G74 2013
    738.092—dc23

2012047601

Roaring Brook Press books may be purchased for business or promotional use. For information on bulk purchases
please contact Macmillan Corporate and Premium Sales Department at (800) 221-7945 x5442 or by email at specialmarkets@macmillan.com.

First Edition 2013
Book design by Jennifer Browne
Printed in China by South China Printing Co. Ltd., Dongguan City, Guangdong Province

1 3 5 7 9 10 8 6 4 2

CONTENTS

Trick photo of George Ohr seeming to stand on his head, c. 1890s.

OUR STORY BEGINS

Biloxi, Mississippi, 1968: The sign read "Ojo's Junk Yard and Machine Shop"—a place to find car parts for an old Model T Ford or a broken down washing machine, not a long lost treasure. Jim Carpenter, an antiques dealer on a buying trip, responded with a cautious yes to an offer from Ojo and his brother Leo to "look at our Daddy's pots." At first glance, all he could see in the dark, tumbledown brick shed were open cartons stacked with more junk. Then he took another look. Before him lay a startling sight—a stash of over 5,000 pieces of pottery, all made by the eccentric Biloxi potter, George Ohr. George always insisted, "My pots are worth their weight in gold," even though, during his lifetime, almost no one wanted them. Now, more than fifty years after his death, it looked as if his words might come true.

There they were, George's "mud babies."

A helter-skelter hodgepodge.

POTS RUFFLED,

crinkled, pinched, and

SWIRLED.

Pots stretched,
BULBOUS,

FOLDED, AND SQUASHED.

A few broken, a few more
chipped and cracked.
And several with
unexpected

MUD DAUBER'S WASP NESTS.

Carpenter knew he had stumbled upon a treasure trove
by a now obscure potter, a master craftsman, who was a
great artist as well. Would the world see what he saw? How
could he convince the Ohr brothers to part with their family
legacy? Who was this George E. Ohr?

10

CHAPTER 1
THE FAMILY BAD BOY

For most of his adult life, folks called George Ohr

A SCALLYWAG

A RASCAL

A BRAGGART

A CLOWN.

He called himself

A GENIUS

AN ARTIST

AN OUTSIDER

A MUD DAUBER

THE MAD POTTER.

This is his story.

He was born in 1857 in Biloxi, Mississippi, a sleepy town on the Gulf of Mexico, where sparkling blue water lured fisherman and sparkling white beaches lured tourists. When George was almost four, the first shots of the Civil War were fired—the northern states, the Union, fighting against the southern states, the Confederacy.

Famous Biloxi Lighthouse, photographed in 1900; a landmark since it was built in 1848.

Fewer than 800 people lived in Biloxi, but it was a seaport and that made it important. Within months, the Union Navy took possession of the town without a battle from the locals and established its base on nearby Ship Island. By then most men of military age had gone off to join the army. Those who remained behind endured a lack of food and supplies, as well as the uncertainty of war.

In 1865, after four years of fierce combat, the Confederacy surrendered. Slavery was abolished in the United States.

George grew up during the war and its aftermath. He always felt out of step, especially with his family.

"Suppose five hen eggs were put under a brood and somebody somewhere made a mistake and got a duck egg in the job lot . . . I'm that duck and no fault of mine."

Being odd man out was fine with George as long as he wasn't ignored. He was the family bad boy, and they were the first to tell him so.

"I had a big load to haul and survived many catastrophes, besides getting all the lickings of the family . . .

"Everything that was ever done wrong . . .

"Or if it did not rain, or rained too much . . .

Above: Biloxi Lighthouse pot, 1895. Made by George, with inscribed decorations by his assistant, Harry Portman. Harry later became the keeper of the Biloxi Lighthouse. Right: Close-up of the back of the Biloxi Lighthouse pot, showing Portman's line sketch of the lighthouse.

"Or the clock wouldn't tick . . .

"Or someone's horse ran away, and 1,000 other things . . ."

All blamed on George!

He went to school and learned to do sums, to read and write. He even spent a winter at a school in New Orleans, ninety miles away. At thirteen, he was finished with classrooms. For a boy expected to earn a living with his hands, that was considered enough formal education.

Horses still provided the chief means of transportation in America. George Sr. was the first blacksmith in Biloxi. He taught his son the trade, heating and hammering metal to make horseshoes, wagon wheels, and fancy ironwork for fences and balconies. George could have gone into business with his father, but he disliked the hot, noisy forge. Besides, they never agreed on anything. Instead

13

Photograph of downtown Biloxi c. 1900.

George helped out at his mother's grocery store and tried mending worn out pots. Nothing suited him.

Tired of arguing with his father, George set out for New Orleans. The only jobs the fourteen-year-old boy could find were at a restaurant in exchange for food and lodging and later at a warehouse that supplied goods for ships. Complaining his bosses overworked and underpaid him, he ran off to sea on a sailing ship. He lasted for one voyage.

George was ready for luck to single him out, but luck seemed to be taking its time. With nothing better in sight, he went home to Biloxi.

CHAPTER 2
LIKE A DUCK IN WATER

By the time a boyhood friend, Joseph Meyer, wrote offering him a job, George had worked in more than fourteen low-paying positions. None lasted very long. Meyer, who owned a small pottery factory in New Orleans, promised to teach him the potter's craft. Meyer needed a helper and George needed a job. He hopped a freight train and for the modest salary of $10 a month signed on to be Meyer's apprentice. It didn't take George long to be hooked.

HE LEARNED TO FORM THE CLAY INTO LONG SAUSAGES AND COIL THEM INTO A POT, TO ROLL THE CLAY FLAT AND CUT OUT SHAPES, OR THIN THE CLAY INTO A THICK LIQUID AND POUR IT INTO A MOLD.

He used all of these methods, but from the beginning his passion was the wheel.

"When I found the potter's wheel I felt it all over like a duck in water."

At age twenty-two, George was handsome and sure of himself—dark-haired with a full, well-groomed moustache and piercing eyes. Shirtsleeves rolled up, a cap perched on his head to keep clay dust out of his eyes, he labored at the potter's wheel, using a foot pedal to make it turn, squishing the wet, slippery mud through his fingers. The faster George

George was proud of his bulging blacksmith arms and often displayed them in photographs.

15

Drawing by William Woodward, 1889. George in the New Orleans Art Pottery studio, working at the wheel.

pumped, the faster the wheel spun. As it revolved, he learned how to use his hands and body to coax a lump of clay into a pot.

After two years with Meyer, George left New Orleans on "a zigzag trip and got as far as Dubuque, Milwaukee, Albany, down the Hudson and zigzag back home." He took advantage of the Civil War push to connect the whole country by rail. Freight trains became his personal jump-on-and-jump-off method of transportation. Like the pioneers, George possessed a very American spirit of adventure, a will to take risks and explore. Naturally his explorations centered on a passion for pots.

He wrote that on his journey, "I sized up every potter and pottery in sixteen states and never missed a show window, illustration, or literary dab since that time, 1881."

Made of clay, ceramics have a history stretching back many thousands of years. The material is both flexible and easily available. Deposits of clay exist in the earth almost all over the world. On George's trip, as well as in his reading, he studied pottery by artisans in varied cultures, from England to China.

Short-term work at some of the folk potteries that dotted America bolstered his meager finances and taught him more tricks of the potter's trade. Yet how would he put these tricks to good use?

"8 to 7" snake jug from the Kirkpatrick Brothers pottery, 1877.

CHAPTER 3

BACK IN BILOXI

Tchoutacabouffa River.

George rowed himself up the Tchoutacabouffa (*CHOO-tah-kah-BUH-fuh*) River with a shovel resting on the bottom of his barge. He needed clay, and here, where the river exposed the soil in veins of yellow, purple, and gray, it lay free for anyone willing to dig. In fact Native American tribes had been mining clay in the same spot for thousands of years. The very name of the river was the Biloxi Indian word for "broken pot." George loaded the mud slabs into a rowboat attached to his barge and steered it back down the river to the dock, where he could shovel the clay into a wagon to take back to his pottery.

With total savings of $26.80, George planned to strike out on his own. Even in 1881, that much money didn't go far. To stretch his budget, George first moved in with his parents, where rent, food, and laundry were free. "I was a dead beat all right." He also was the original do-it-yourselfer.

"AS I WAS AN EX-BLACKSMITH, I MADE THE IRON WORK, THE CLAY MILL AND POTTERS WHEEL. MY CAPITAL WAS ALL PUT INTO BRICK FOR THE KILN. GOT HOLD OF SOME PINE TREES AND HAD 'EM SAWED UP AND RAFTED

George's second pottery, c. 1894.

THE LUMBER DOWN THE RIVER. HAULED THE LUMBER MYSELF AND BUILT THE FIRST SHOP ALL ALONE."

When his father found out George had swiped all his tools, "he kicked like a circus mule but Mamma said, 'Let the boy go on and watch him.'"

The building was not much more than a shack with a clay mill outside, to clean sand and gravel out of the river clay, and a wood-fueled kiln to fire his pots. George was in business, or as he punned, a Pot-Ohr. He made usable objects he could sell to local homeowners—anything they needed from tiles, stove flues, and water jugs, to flower pots and vases. For visitors to Biloxi he made cheap knickknacks and souvenirs, which he called his "trinkets," such as piggy banks, inkwells, and match holders.

Bowl with folded alteration, c. 1897–1900.

The Blacksmith Potter, as he was dubbed, pushed a handmade cart from door to door and peddled his goods around town. George told the townsfolk there was a magical substance in river mud that allowed him to make such charming wares.

He told tourists that his glittering glazes were due to the fire of the kiln. In truth the silver streaks, deep reds, and tangerines that curled like flames around the pots were the result of his constant experiments. He ground and mixed concoctions of lead, sand, and various colorants. Brushed on a fired pot, this mixture dried dull and flat. After a second firing, the colors blazed into life.

In Biloxi's balmy, tropical climate, George was surrounded by the ever-shifting blues of the Gulf of Mexico and

Vase, 1893–1909.

WORLD'S INDUSTRIAL & COTTON CENTENNIAL EXPOSITION AT NEW ORLEANS, LA.

DIMENSIONS, SIX HUNDRED BY ONE HUNDRED & NINETY FOUR FEET.   CENTRE ARRANGED TO SHOW 20,000 PLATES OF FRUIT.

HORTICULTURAL HALL.

the lush colors of flowering trees—chinaberry, apple, peach, plum, and willow—that dotted the streets and lawns of the town. Fleets of shrimp boats and steel gray oyster draggers lined the docks. Roads paved with pearly crushed oyster shells gleamed in the sunlight. All these brilliant colors found their way into his glazes.

George cast some of his pitchers and planters by pouring thinned clay into plaster molds, drying and firing it, an efficient way to create cheap pottery to sell. He also used molds for a few of the handles and spouts for teapots. These practical items paid the bills. His pride, however, lay in the original work he turned out on the wheel.

In 1884, with high hopes, George chose 600 pots to display at the World's Industrial and Cotton Centennial in New Orleans, an international fair to promote the city and the cotton industry. The Civil War had shattered the economy and humbled the reputation of the South. Proud residents of New Orleans resolved to bounce back.

Large urn, 1892, constructed in three pieces: a combination of molded and thrown sections, one of two known to exist.

Since travel to far-off places was difficult and expensive, people looked to world's fairs to offer imaginary glimpses into distant lands and to see the latest fads and inventions. Diversions such as ragtime music, excursions on the Mississippi River, and working models of electric streetcars entertained the crowds.

Assigned a booth in the Machinery Hall at the 249-acre fair, George set up a portable wheel where he sang southern songs and whirled clay into pots. Spectators happily gawked at his shenanigans but kept their money in their pockets. After the fair, the man George hired to cart the unsold pots back to Biloxi stole them instead.

"It turned out to be nobody's business and everybody's pottery," quipped George.

For the next few years he caught boxcars back and forth from Biloxi to New Orleans to pick up extra jobs. It's not too surprising that he met his future bride, Josephine, at the Biloxi train depot. They married in 1886, and George settled down to responsible family life.

He built a bigger place to include a showroom filled floor to ceiling with pots, but saved money by leaving out the glass in the windows. He painted the wood frame building an eye-catching pink. George's early pottery was traditional in style, symmetrical with thick walls, and simple glazes.

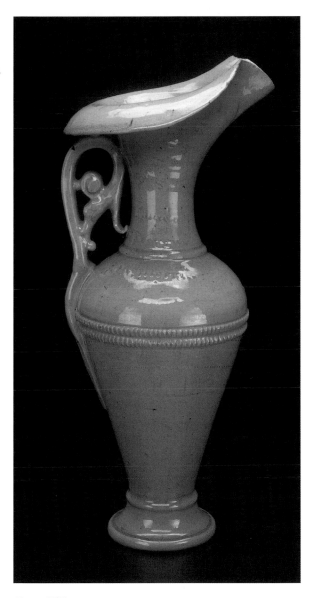

Ewer, 1891.

21

Oil painting of George at the potter's wheel by William Woodward, 1889. Joseph Meyer is the figure in the background.

Soon a variety of his wares from jugs and garden urns to the occasional umbrella stand lined a ledge under the roof and spilled into the front yard. Yet business was slow. Worried about money, he went back to New Orleans to assist Joseph Meyer again. Meyer had opened a studio to furnish pottery for the Ladies' Decorative Art League. Jobs for "proper ladies" outside the home were limited. Decorating ceramics offered them an acceptable way to earn a living. After George threw and fired pots—the dirty work—the Woodward brothers, two distinguished professors of art, taught the young women to paint them. They called these decorative objects, festooned with flowers or dragons, "art pottery."

Three decorative clay shoes. The one on the left is by Joseph Meyer, the other two are by George.

George never graduated from high school, let alone attended an art school. Now he found himself surrounded by a sophisticated, well-educated group of artists, teachers, and students from nearby Tulane College, who discussed ceramics, not as useful tableware, but as an art form.

At the Decorative Art League, rows of young women in starched white smocks glazed the vases. George played the role of a picturesque character, flirting and showing off his blacksmith muscles. Curious and observant, he also absorbed the artistic scene around him.

Meyer's pottery shop eventually closed and George backtracked to Biloxi. Before returning home, he made a decision. He might behave like a country bumpkin, but he was no longer content to make only dishes, pipes, fanciful clay shoes, and pots in the style of his mentor Joseph Meyer. He always had faith in his mechanical ability as a potter and now a spark had ignited his imagination.

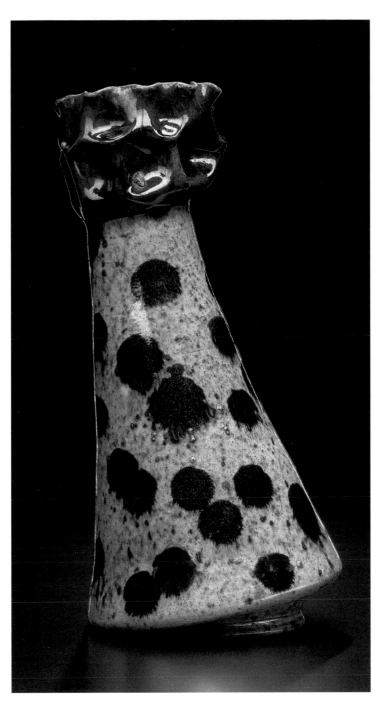

Tilted vase, c. 1897–1900. The tilted vase looks light-hearted, like a leaning tower or the long spotted neck of a giraffe.

His hands expert at the wheel, his mind filled with dreams of beautiful objects, he would let his creativity fly.

George's self-invented "Mad Potter" persona was in full swing. With his long mustache twirled up around his ears and his beard neatly tucked in his shirt, he lured tourists to his demonstrations.

"THIS IS WHAT I WILL DO ON MY WHEEL— BLINDFOLDED—

TURN A JUG, PUT A CORNCOB STOPPER ON IT, CHANGE THE CORNCOB INTO A FUNNEL—

HAVE THE FUNNEL DISAPPEAR AND HAVE A JAR—

CHANGE THE JAR INTO AN URN AND HALF A DOZEN OTHER SHAPES

Above: Puzzle mug, c. 1900.
Right: The clockface vase, c. 1898, with incised decorations by Harry Portman.

AND TURN ANYTHING THAT ANYONE IN THE U.S.A. CAN MENTION THAT IS CYLINDRICAL ON THAT POTTER'S WHEEL."

Sometimes he scratched the customer's name and date on a mug or a short rowdy verse on a damp piggy bank. Bystanders laughed at his antics and bought his clay shoes, inkwells, or coins, but not his "art ware."

George loved performing—he played coronet in the town band and acted in plays. Using trick photography, he posed as twins or upside down. His sense of humor also came out in his novelty ware. In a puzzle mug, one of George's most successful items, the puzzle is how to drink from it without dribbling water from the holes. The handle acts as a straw. While holding a finger over the hole

Above: Green teapot with original triangular clay price tag, 1900–1909, featured on the Antiques Roadshow *in 2011.*

Below: Wrinkled vase, c. 1897–1900. The undulating form brings to mind a sea creature or a topographical map.

Above: George posing in a trick photograph, 1905.

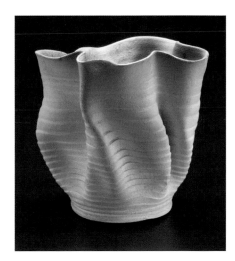

Top: Four low pots, c. 1895–1900.
Above: One of George's signature stamps.

underneath the handle, one sips from a small opening in the rim that connects to a hole in the bottom of the mug.

Beneath the flash and dash, George had a deeper purpose. New Orleans changed his view of himself, and the sign on his shop also changed, from Biloxi Pottery to Biloxi Art Pottery. That three-letter word "Art" made all the difference.

George vowed to leave his mark—not just the stamp on the bottom of his pots, Geo E. Ohr, Biloxi, Miss, but also, on the form, each pot inventive and novel, made by the artist's hand. **"NO TWO ALIKE"** became his motto.

CHAPTER 4
FIRE

October 12, 1894: The first flames licked out of the Bijou Oyster Bar. By the time the town's night watchman saw them, the fire had spread fast through downtown Biloxi. The volunteer fire department, of which George was a member, could do nothing but watch helplessly. Offices, bungalows, the Opera House, the laundry, the grocery store owned by George's mother, and his own house and studio with the high brick-roofed kiln went up in smoke.

Earlier that year, George and Josephine had lost their four-year-old son, Asa, the second of their children to die. They mourned a boy barely old enough to dodge his father's footsteps around the pottery yard.

Now, in a matter of hours disaster overtook them again—their house and workplace were reduced to ashes. The big kiln had a hole in one side. Worst of all, the charred remains of George's pottery lay in the rubble. Everything he worked so hard to build had vanished.

The next morning George bravely posed for a photograph taken next to his battered kiln, two of his children, Leo and Clo Lucinda, standing in front of him. George tenderly collected

Two "burned babies," c. 1892–94.

The day after the fire. George and his children in front of the big kiln.

the soot-encrusted remains of the pots he had called his "mud babies." He renamed them his "killed babies," never to be thrown away.

Since there was no insurance, George offered one-dollar coupons to be exchanged for merchandise when he rebuilt the pottery. He had no trouble getting the $800 he needed. After all, he was an established tourist attraction. In an article in the *New Orleans Daily Picayune*, the reporter had listed two things not to be missed in Biloxi: the local watercress served for breakfast, lunch, and dinner and the Ohr Art Pottery.

Soon after the fire, George constructed a small house for his growing family. In the next twelve years, he and Josephine would crowd that house with children. George mischievously named them Leo, Clo, Lio, Oto, Flo, Zio, Ojo, and Geo. Their first names were also their initials. George prized word play, not only referring to himself as a Pot-Ohr, but also calling the shop a Pot-Ohr-E.

*Top: Five red vases, c. 1895–1910
Left: George and Josphine with some of their children. Two children in the front row are holding pots.*

Left: Near the top of the building is a shoo-fly, an open level high enough to keep away the flies and catch a breeze.

George next designed a larger studio complete with a five story wooden tower topped off by a flagpole. Since it was the tallest building in town, no one could miss it, which was just what George wanted. On shelves around the kiln yard he arranged his "killed babies."

George's signs hung all over town, "Greatest Art Potter on Earth. You prove the contrary." He cheerfully described himself as a "rankey krankey solid individualist," a self-styled American maverick "born free and patriotic, blowing my own bugle." His fanciful personality made such an impression that he even inspired a novel—*The Wonderful Wheel*—whose main character, a potter with his mustache draped over his ears, was based on George. No sightseer to the Gulf Coast could miss a trip to the Biloxi Art Pottery.

Above: Wide double-necked form, c. 1897–1900. George's inventive dark metallic glaze and helmet-like shape give the piece a sinister look.

CHAPTER 5
"NO TWO ALIKE"

The fire gave George a new sense of urgency. Before the destruction, he had begun to experiment with shapes. Just as the new studio was larger, more extravagant, so were his pots. In a creative frenzy, he manipulated the still wet clay into even more pronounced curves and free-flowing forms. Though he continued with his novelty items, in the next few years he also made thousands of his "no two alike" pots.

To George there were artistic reasons for stressing the handmade, unique quality of his pottery. He believed in the ideals of the Arts and Crafts movement, popular with architects and artisans at the time. It celebrated the notion of a single craftsman, working by hand. George lived by these values.

Yet he was on the wrong side of history. By the turn of the twentieth century, the Industrial Revolution brought many innovative ways to manufacture goods in America. The day of the individual craftsman was over. Well-known art potteries began to mass-produce their wares. For example, at the celebrated Rookwood Company in Cincinnati, Ohio, five

Ducktail pitcher, c. 1898–1910.

workers made pottery molds and cast the pots, others painted them, and the rest fired them. George scorned manufactured pottery as production line, not art. Rookwood's finely painted landscapes and floral designs held no interest for him.

He also continued to tinker with his glaze formulas. The Ohr children would watch him add filings of iron, brass, lead, and copper to the mixtures. His glazes reflected the natural world, from the rough, striated texture of bark to the glistening ripples of a waterfall. He viewed his surroundings with an artist's eye.

Yet, as much as people might rave about his distinctive glazes, it was the shapes he created that mattered most to George. His inspiration came from manipulating the clay itself.

The paper-thin vessels, altered both on and off the wheel, appeared alive and breathing with a sense of the maker's touch.

He might **RUFFLE OR FLUTE THE EDGES,** **TWIST THE NECK,** **MAKE A BORDER OF HIS THUMBPRINTS,**

FASHION CURVING HANDLES,

TWIST, WRING, PUMMEL, AND FOLD THE WALLS,

until each pot,
although contorted,
seemed to twirl
in space.

The effect was witty, rhythmic, and sensual.

They weren't containers to store foodstuffs or pitchers to pour lemonade. George's pots were sculptures, three-dimensional works of art. "Shapes come to the potter as verses come to the poet," he wrote.

From 1903 on, perhaps thumbing his nose at those who admired his colors,

he concentrated on crafting a series of unglazed or bisque-fired vessels, his most experimental shapes yet. George could make magic. Yet Rookwood and other potteries won medals at the fairs, while the judges passed right by Pot-Ohr-E.

Only a few critics and other potters realized

37

Scalloped form, c. 1897–1900.

what George was doing. Most called him a show-off and disliked his weird forms and outrageous colors.

A respected potter admitted George had skill but wrote, "[H]e used it to make rubbish and thus diminishes the whole value of pottery of his kind."

George fought back. He printed handbills boasting of his prowess and superior craftsmanship, "unequaled, unrivalled, undisputed." How could anyone who behaved so flamboyantly be taken seriously as an artist? George said, "I found out long ago that it paid me to act that way."

His brash advertisements and self-promotion might fit into the culture of the twenty-first century, but, in his day, it turned off the very people he wanted to impress. One of his more insightful fans wrote, "Mr. Ohr is by no means a crank,

Pitcher with snake handle, c. 1895–96. George's decorative snakes were much less realistic than the ones on the Kirkpatrick's jug. See page 16.

but is a naturally bright, even brilliant man, who has been led into the belief that the way for him to attain publicity is through the channel of preposterous advertising, and the signs which he placed round Biloxi do him more harm than good."

George could not change his personality, any more than he could change his art to please others. He might bluster and pose, but he put his sensitive soul into his unmistakable pots. Perhaps "unmistakable" was his biggest problem. His work just didn't fit in with the times.

Despite the rejections, he developed his own grand—some

*Left: Two vases, c. 1897–1900
and c. 1895–96.*

might say grandiose—vision. His art ware,
he insisted, must be sold to one museum or
collector. He made it hard for the occasional
daring collector to buy his work at all. The
prices he asked for favorite pieces cost as much
as an ordinary laborer's paycheck for a month.
He often concocted little tests. A prospective
buyer had to assure George that he was indeed
a great artist or he rudely canceled the sale.

Ambitious, he embraced the American
Dream of success through grit and hard work.
Yet he yearned for fame, not wealth. Without a
bit of shame, he said, "Every genius is in debt."

Above: Totem-like form, c. 1897–1900.

CHAPTER 6
THE LAST HURRAH

1904. Tempting odors of cotton candy, hot dogs, and hamburgers filled the air of the wondrous Louisiana Purchase Exhibition, popularly known as the St. Louis World's Fair. The allure of newfangled foods, along with exotic sideshows and exhibits from sixty-two foreign nations and forty-three of the then forty-five states, brought over 19 million visitors. This was a fair meant to amaze and impress, and George wanted to be there amazing people too.

With several hundred of his "mud babies" in tow, he hoped that at last people of taste and refinement would discover his work. Along with such sights as an Irish village, a huge manmade circular waterfall, and an Asian temple complete with

elephants and camels, there were many displays of American and European ceramics.

All the fairs George attended gave him an opportunity to see the designs of other potteries and to compare his own work. This time he won a silver medal, the highest award he ever received, but, as usual, no one bought his art ware.

When the exposition closed, he was so broke he couldn't afford to go home. He might have been bull-headed, but he was also industrious. Hired by the St. Louis school system to train teachers to use the potter's wheel, he managed to muster enough cash to buy a ticket back to Biloxi.

Above: Pink ewer, c. 1897–1900.

Above: Two striped bisque vessels, c. 1898–1910. George called the mix of two or more colors of clay "scrottled."

As much as George loved traveling to fairs around the country, he knew those days were over. What had all the solitary years of hard labor brought him? From then on, George stayed put. Every once in a while his name came up in pottery journals. Galleries in New York or Washington, D.C., included his work in group shows. The Smithsonian Museum received a box of Ohr vessels for their ceramics collection. They didn't return George's gift, but they didn't display it either.

George in retirement.

When a potters' association requested a few pots for an exhibition, George shipped them off with a note, "I send you four pieces, but it is as easy to pass judgment on my productions from four pieces as it would be to take four lines from Shakespeare and guess the rest."

Back home, George had other problems. After his parents died, he inherited property he shared equally with his brother and sisters. They wanted to sell, he didn't, and matters grew ugly. The opposing lawyers said George was crazy. He objected. Yes, he called himself The Mad Potter, but that was just theatrics. Soon he was summoned to court for a humiliating lunacy hearing. "[A]fter diligently examining witnesses on oath, and after personal examination of said George E. Ohr," the jury found "that the said George E. Ohr is not insane."

Some might call George immature and childish, but that side of his character went along with being joyful and uninhibited in his creative life.

Perhaps tired of the struggle to be recognized, he retired from actively making ceramics in 1910. After choosing some pots to keep around the house, he stuffed the rest into crates and stored them in a rickety attic. With typical bravado he instructed his family not to sell them for fifty years.

Meanwhile the Pot-Ohr-E was finished. He handed his building over to his sons. In 1903, Henry Ford's first Model T Fords had rolled off the assembly line in Detroit. Automobiles were no longer just toys for the rich. The sons took down the tower, cut a large door in the side, and put up their own sign: "Ohr Boys Auto Repairing Shop."

George and his sons on some of Biloxi's first motorcycles in front of the "Ohr Boys Auto Repairing shop."

His neighbors grew used to the sight of George, his long white beard flying in the wind, tearing down the beach on his motorcycle. Until the wee hours of the night, The Mad Potter sat up scribbling page after page of his rambling thoughts—jokes, puns, poems, and tirades on life and art.

He died of cancer in 1918 at the age of sixty-one. His wife, Josephine, continued to offer pots for sale, but there was not much interest. His grandchildren and great-grandchildren used a few bowls as targets for their BB guns. Possibly still angry that, as a boy, his father insisted he fetch and carry at the pottery, his oldest surviving son Leo took all of George's papers out in the yard and burned them. For the next five decades, most of George's work stayed hidden away, gathering dust, rattling from the rumble of passing freight trains.

At last a kind of miracle happened.

Jim Carpenter, that antiques dealer from New Jersey, appeared on the scene. When he saw those crates crammed full of pottery, Carpenter must have felt as if he had discovered vessels containing decades of lost time. Pots that seemed outrageous back in 1910 looked fresh and modern in the 1970s.

After more than two years of negotiations with George's heirs, Carpenter

finally bought the long-forgotten Ohr art ware for around fifty thousand dollars and hauled it north to clean off, shine up, and sell.

As word spread of a dramatic "new" potter practically unknown to the art world, interest grew. George's pots had survived to tell his story. Famous artists, collectors, museum curators—everybody wanted one.

Pieces sold at auction. Eighty-four thousand dollars for a George E. Ohr vase. One hundred and thirty-three thousand. More. What might have pleased The Mad Potter most of all were the contemporary artists influenced by his work. But beyond even his wildest dreams, Frank Gehry, one of America's greatest architects, designed a museum for the work of the Ohr family bad boy. A museum of curving shapes, gleaming in the Biloxi sun, built in honor of George E. Ohr, one of America's greatest art potters.

Would he be shocked?
George expected it all along.

"I AM MAKING POTS FOR ART SAKE,
THE FUTURE GENERATION AND . . .
FOR MY OWN SATISFACTION, BUT WHEN I'M GONE . . .
MY WORK WILL BE PRIZED, HONORED AND CHERISHED."

THE OHR-O'KEEFE MUSEUM OF ART

By the 1990s, Biloxi was thriving economically as a center on the Gulf Coast for the seafood industry and tourism. It was time to celebrate its cultural history by building a museum for Biloxi's native son, George Ohr, the visionary artist and eccentric. At first there was resistance to the idea. Some people didn't like the potter's art ware. Others didn't know who he was, even though his pottery was sought after by collectors from New York to Los Angeles. For years, the small library in Biloxi housed a collection of George Ohr's pottery. Why spend the money for a new museum?

But Jerry O'Keefe, the former mayor, pledged a million dollars to build a museum to be named the Ohr-O'Keefe Museum of Art in memory of his wife. He would raise the additional funds as well. Eventually public opinion turned positive.

O'Keefe told the committee he wanted the building to be bold like the works of George Ohr. America's boldest architect, Frank Gehry, known for his soaring sculptural designs, was a perfect choice. Although a century separated their careers, both were masters of unconventional forms. What Gehry called Ohr's "wiggly shapes" seemed very much akin to his own. When O'Keefe showed him a site filled with old oak trees overlooking the Gulf of Mexico. Gehry knew this was the perfect spot for the museum.

Staircase to shoo-fly.

of their survival and determination. Now the five structures designed by Gehry and rebuilt amidst the tall oaks invite visitors to move from one skylight space to another or to linger outside on the brick courtyard. One can climb a double staircase to two shoofly terraces at the top of the trees, a nod by Gehry to the architecture of the Old South. There is a gallery devoted to African-American art, as well as spaces to exhibit the works of other artists of the region. George Ohr's pottery is proudly displayed on shelves in the concrete and stainless steel pods. Once George Ohr called himself "the potter who was." Now the world knows him as "the potter who is."

"We made a model of the site, including the trees," said Gehry, "and that's how we realized we couldn't make the building as one. We started dancing with the trees."

But in 2005, just as the museum planned to open, tragedy struck. Hurricane Katrina, with winds over 175 miles an hour, bludgeoned the southern coast of Mississippi. In Biloxi, the high winds and flooding caused a tidal wave to lift a gambling barge, the size of a football field, off its moorings. The steel barge floated off the beach, across the highway, and flattened the museum buildings. Fortunately the Ohr pottery was stored at the library in containers. The hurricane left a devastated city in its wake.

O'Keefe and his group lobbied hard to get the museum rebuilt. They hoped it would inspire a community that had lost so much to renew itself. In 2007, they erected stainless steel pods as a symbol

THE PLEASANT REED INTERPRETIVE CENTER

Pleasant Reed was a former slave who lived in Biloxi at the same time as George Ohr. Pleasant, a skilled carpenter, built this modest bungalow with money he earned as a free man. Now on the grounds of the Ohr-O'Keefe Museum, the cottage, reconstructed since Hurricane Katrina, is used as a learning center for the history of African-Americans on the Gulf Coast.

HOW TO LOOK AT A POT

Quintessential teapot, c. 1897–1900.

WHAT DO WE SEE? Here is a teapot with a spout shaped like an open-mouthed snake and a bright red glaze covered with pock marks. The label tells us it is 7 3/16 inches high by 7 1/8 inches wide.

SENSORY WORDS describe qualities in an artwork that remind us of things we can see, feel, taste, touch, or smell. Here are some sensory words that come to mind when we look closely at this artwork in terms of color, form, line, and texture. The **TEXTURE** is blistery and splotchy with ragged, notchlike craters, rough to the touch. The overall **COLOR** is a mottled, orangey red with a pattern of irregular gray green marks. The **FORM** is unusual for a teapot. The bulbous-shaped body is indented. The **LINES** of the handle look like a curving ribbon. Ohr crimped two small projections on it.

HOW WAS IT MADE? Indents on the body of the pot are typical of Ohr's style. He might have used his thumbprints or the sides of his hands to push the wet clay in after shaping it on the wheel. Although traditionally handles were made to be strong and functional, this handle looks delicate and decorative. Probably he cut the clay into a strip and pinched it into a handle. As a blacksmith who forged ornamental iron gates and fences, George found inspiration in these shapes.

WHAT IS THE FEELING EXPRESSED? The bright-colored, fanciful handle and the spout that looks like a comical sea serpent give this piece a whimsical feeling. Although a teapot is a usable object, Ohr's teapot with its thin walls and fragile handle is more a decorative object, not really meant to be used for hot tea.

AND HOW TO "BOSS" ONE OF YOUR OWN
(AS GEORGE WOULD SAY)

Here are some of the steps you will take. Center a lump of clay on the round potter's wheel. Work the pedal attached to the wheel so that the wheel starts spinning. Use your feet to pump in an even rhythm. Press your thumbs into the middle of the clay as the wheel spins. You will make a hole with your thumbs, and your fingers will shape the walls of the pot. Slowly the form grows under your hands like a living thing. Use your thumbs to thin the walls of the pot. Remember, clay follows the motions of the body as well as the hands. (And don't forget to keep your foot pumping to spin the wheel.)

Throwing a pot is a tricky business. When you're satisfied with the shape, take it off the wheel.

Trim off the excess clay. Let the pot dry, then fire it in a kiln (an oven made especially to bake or fire clay.) The temperature can be 1,700 or more degrees Fahrenheit. This first firing removes excess moisture, so the pot can be glazed without breaking.

When your piece is done, let it cool. It will be hard and slightly porous, like a clay flowerpot.

If you want a colorful pot with waterproof coating, paint it with a glaze. You can buy a glaze or make one according to your own secret recipe. Before you begin to glaze, smooth the surface with sandpaper and sponge it off. You might paint it one color or a combination of colors. Sometimes George splattered the glaze with a brush to achieve a mottled surface. After the glaze dries, it will look drab, but don't worry. Put the pot into the kiln to fire again. This time the temperature is even hotter. Let the pot cool again, dust it off, and you're done.

BIBLIOGRAPHY

Biloxi Historical Society, www.biloxihistoricalsociety.org.

Blasberg, Robert W. 1973. *George E. Ohr and His Biloxi Art Pottery*. Port Jervis, New York: Jim Carpenter. Reprinted in 2008 by the Ohr-O'Keefe Museum of Art with a new foreword and notes by the Ohr-O'Keefe Museum of Art.

Clark, Garth, Robert A. Ellison, Jr., and Eugene Hecht. 1989. *The Mad Potter of Biloxi: The Art and Life of George E. Ohr*. New York: Abbeville Press.

Dale, Ron, ed. 1983. *The George E. Ohr Exhibition Catalogue*, University of Mississippi. Connecticut: JO-D Books.

Eidelberg, Martin. 1987. *From Our Active Clay: Art Pottery from the Collections of the American Ceramic Arts Society*. New York: Turn of the Century Editions.

Ellison, Robert A. 2006. *George Ohr, Art Potter: Apostle of Individuality*. London: Scala Publishers Limited.

Ellison, Robert A., and Rosaire Appel (interview with authors). February 2012, New York.

Greenberg, Jan, and Sandra Jordan. 2000. *Frank O. Gehry: Outside In*. New York: DK Publishing.

Gowdy, Marjorie, Anna Harris, and Elaine Levin. 2007. *Goerge Ohr Rising: The Emergence of an American Master*. Biloxi, Mississippi: Ohr-O'Keefe Museum of Art.

Hecht, Eugene. 1994. *After the Fire: George Ohr: An American Genius*. Lambertville, New Jersey: Arts and Crafts Quarterly Press.

Hecht, Eugene. 1993. "George E. Ohr: The Mad Potter of Biloxi." *The Magazine of the Mississippi Museum of Art* 4, no. 1.

Hecht, Eugene, and Carolyn Hecht (interview with authors). March 2012, New York.

Lippert, Ellen. January 2009. "George Ohr in His Nineteenth Century Context: The Mad Potter Reconsidered." Unpublished diss., Case Western Reserve University.

Mississippi Public Broadcasting. 1993. *George Ohr: The Mad Potter of Biloxi* (documentary).

Mohr, Richard D. November/December 2000. "George Ohr: The Letters, A Series—Part 1." *The Journal of the American Pottery Association* 16.

Mohr, Richard D. 2009. *Pottery, Politics, Art: George Ohr and the Brothers Kirkpatrick*. Urbana and Chicago: University of Illinois Press.

Ohr, George E. 1901. "Some Facts in the History of a Unique Personality: Autobiography of George E. Ohr, the Biloxi Potter." *Crockery and Glass Journal*, 54.

Ohr-O'Keefe Museum of Art, www.georgeohr.org.

Scholl, Dennis (writer, producer, director). 2012. *Dancing with the Trees* (documentary).

Watson, Bruce. February 2004. "The Mad Potter of Biloxi." *Smithsonian*.

NOTES

OUR STORY BEGINS . . .

9: Biloxi: The Mississippi town was named after the Native American Biloxi tribe that lived in the area. Spanish explorers claimed the land, but the first European settlement in 1699 was French. In 1817, Mississippi became the twentieth state to join the Union.

9: Tales of how Jim Carpenter (and his wife, Mim) discovered the pots and brought them into the world vary as great stories in the oral tradition often do. Watson, Biloxi Historical, Ellison 2012, Hecht 2012, Clark, Mississippi Public Broadcasting

9: "My pots are worth their weight . . ." Hecht 2012, Clark, p.32

9: There they were, George's "mud babies." Clark, p.123

CHAPTER 1

11: A mud dauber: a colloquial name for any one of three different kinds of wasps who make their nests of mud.

11: The American Civil War lasted from April 12, 1861, when Confederate forces fired on and captured the Union-held Fort Sumter, in South Carolina, until the surrender of the Confederacy to the Union Army at Appomattox Court House in Virginia, April 9, 1865 (although fighting continued after that date until the news caught up with the soldiers). When the Union forces captured Ship Island (near Biloxi) in December, 1861, they wanted to use it as a base to attack the large port of New Orleans in nearby Louisiana. The 2nd Louisiana Native Guard volunteers, one of the first black U.S. combat units to fight in the Civil War, was based there.

12: Slavery was abolished: President Lincoln issued the Emancipation Proclamation in January 1863 which, by executive order (with some exceptions), freed slaves in the ten states that had seceded from the Union. Slavery was made illegal by the Thirteenth Amendment in December 1865.

12: "I have a notion . . .": Ohr, p. 23

12–13: "I had a big load . . .": Ohr, p. 24

CHAPTER 2

15: Joseph Meyer . . .: Joseph Fortune Meyer, potter and artist (1848–1931)

15: "When I found . . .": Ohr, p. 26

16: "I sized up every . . .": Ohr, p. 26

16: "a zigzag trip . . .": Ohr, p. 26

16: In his travels . . .: George would later echo his take on the shape of a Greek urn or the glaze on a Chinese peach blow vase. His real love seems to have been the French potter Bernard Palissy (c.1510–1590), an eccentric French potter and scientist who covered his vases with reptiles. George occasionally put a snake on a vase, but he couldn't be said to have been influenced by Palissy. Still, he identified with the Frenchman and now and then referred to himself as the "American Palissy." Clark, pp. 70–75

16: Short-term work . . .: In pre-industrial America, there were many local potteries, usually situated near deposits of excellent clay. We know George visited the Kirkpatrick brothers' Anna Pottery company in Anna, Illinois, because his inscription has been found on pottery from there.

CHAPTER 3

17: the Biloxi Indian word . . .: The Biloxi tribe that existed in 1699 when the first Europeans settled in the area was a numerous native American people probably descended from the earlier Mississippian culture and mound builders. The date of habitation in Mississippi and Louisiana keeps being pushed back as more discoveries are made, but is now thought to be 7,000 or more years BCE. Much decimated in numbers by disease, the Biloxi are now federally recognized as the Tunica-Biloxi tribe.

17: George loaded the mud . . .: The description of digging mud comes from Hecht 1994, p. 3; Blasberg, p. 5; and MPB interview with Ojo Ohr. The descriptions vary slightly, but they all agree George did it himself for more than twenty years.

17: "I was a deadbeat . . .": Ohr, p. 26

17: "As I was an ex-blacksmith . . .": Ohr, p. 26

18: "he kicked like a circus . . .": Ohr, p. 25

20: lush colors of flowering trees . . .: Clark, p. 17

21: "It turned out . . .": Ohr, p. 25

22: the Woodward brothers . . .: William Woodward (1859–1939) and his brother Ellsworth Woodward (1861–1939) were two Massachusetts-born artists who became important painters in late-nineteenth century New Orleans. Ellsworth Woodward was one of the founders of Newcomb Pottery.

23: Now he found himself . . .: Influence of the Woodwards and others of their circle on George Ohr, from an interview with Gene Hecht.

23: from nearby Tulane College . . .: Tulane University, a Louisiana university for men, was established as a medical school in 1834 and became a full university in 1947. The H. Sophie Newcomb Memorial College for women was founded in 1886 as a "coordinate college" with Tulane.

23: Meyer's pottery shop . . .: Newcomb Pottery made pottery for profit from 1895–1940. William and Ellsworth Woodward started it at Newcomb College, and Joseph Meyer and his assistants did the heavy work of throwing the pots in the early years.

25: "This is what I will . . .": Mohr 2000, p. 18

28: "No two alike . . .": Clark, p. 74

CHAPTER 4

29: The first flames . . .: Description of the fire. Hecht 1994, pp.1–2

29: Earlier that year . . .: The Ohr children. Ella Louise 1897, Asa Eugene 1889–1893, Leo Ernest 1889–1920, Clo Lucinda 1892–1989, Lio Irwin 1893–1914, Oto Theodore 1895–1982, Flo/Lucagina 1898–1900, Zio Ignatius 1900–1904, Ojo Julius 1903–1986, Geo E. 1906–1974.

31: "The potter stands . . .": Hecht 1994, p. 8

32: a"rankey krankey solid individualist . . .": Blasberg, p. 18

32: American maverick "born free and patriotic . . ." Blasberg, p. 14

CHAPTER 5

35: Arts and Crafts movement: The movement, which started in England and had as one of its chief proponents the artist, designer, and writer William Morris, quickly spread to the United States. The philosophy of the movement valued individual creativity and good design as a way to improve society.

35: at the celebrated Rookwood Company . . .: Rookwood is a famous pottery started in Cincinnati, Ohio, in 1880 by Maria Storer. It is still in existence.

37: "Shapes come . . .": Ellison 2006, p. 57

38: A respected fellow potter . . . was Charles Fergus Binnes, who, among other things, was the founder of the New York State College of Ceramics: Clark, p. 182

38: "I found out long . . .": Clark, p. 136

38: "Mr. Ohr is by no means . . .": Clark, p. 136

CHAPTER 6

43: "I send you . . .": Clark, p. 34

43: Soon he was summoned to court . . .: The entry on the website of the Biloxi Historical Society says that the two businessmen who had purchased property from the rest of the family had questioned George's sanity and took him to court. They later bought the property at public auction for less than its value.

43: "[A]fter diligently examining . . .": Hecht 1994, pp. 28–29

44: Possibly still angry . . .: Leo was quoted as saying that he hated the fact that his father had made him work at the pottery when he was a boy. Did he burn the papers out of hostility or to keep family secrets? No one knows the answer.

44: For the next six decades . . .: The photographic evidence suggests no one bothered to wrap or protect the pots, but his children did move them several times to keep them safer.

45: One hundred and thirty-three thousand: Scholl

45: More: Hecht (interview with authors)

46: "I am making pots for art's sake . . ." Ellison 2006, p. 169

THE OHR-O'KEEFE MUSEUM OF ART

47: Ohr's "wiggly shapes" . . .: Scholl

48: "We made a model of the site . . .": Scholl

48: But in 2005 . . .: Information about the history of the museum: Scholl

48: "the potter who was.": Dale, p.25

THE PLEASANT REED INTERPRETIVE CENTER

48: Pleasant Reed . . .: *Ohr-O'Keefe Museum of Art* (magazine), a celebration of art and architecture, November, 2010.

PICTURE CREDITS

Every effort has been made to obtain permission for the use of this material.

Since George Ohr did not inventory his pottery, it has been the job of experts in the field to measure, date, and assign titles to identify published pieces.

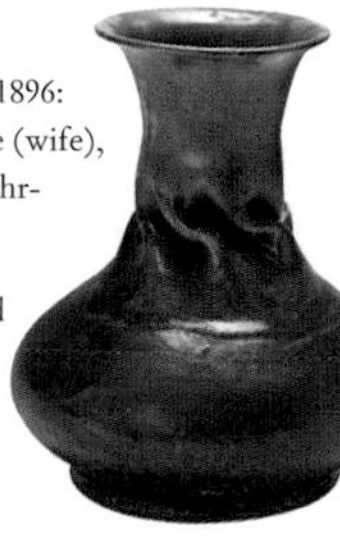

Endpapers: Ohr family, April 1896: George, Lio, Leo, Clo, Josephine (wife), and baby Oto, courtesy of the Ohr-O'Keefe Museum of Art.

Contents: Pitcher from Burned Babies Collection, c. 1893, approximately 2–4 in. (h), courtesy of the Ohr-O'Keefe Museum of Art.

8: Trick photo of George Ohr, courtesy of the Ohr-O'Keefe Museum of Art.

9: Three bisque pots, c. 1898–1910, all 4–4 15/16 in. (h), collection of/photographed by Robert A. Ellison, Jr.

10: Petticoat vase (top right), c. 1899, 7 ¾ in. (h) x 4 ¾ in. (w); Vase with in-body-twist (center), c. 1900, 6 in. (h) x 3 ¼ in. (w); Vase (top left), c. 1900, 5 in. (h) x 4 in. (w). Courtesy of the Ohr-O'Keefe Museum of Art. Totem-like form (bottom right), c. 1897–1900, 7 1/16 in. (h); Mud-dauber bisque vase (bottom left), c. 1898–1910, 8 ⅛ in. (h) x 8 in. (w). Collection of/photographed by Robert A. Ellison, Jr.

12: Biloxi Lighthouse, courtesy of Prints and Photographs, Library of Congress.

13: Biloxi Lighthouse pot, c. 1895, 9 ¼ in (h) x 8 ½ in (w); Close up of Biloxi Lighthouse pot, c. 1895. Courtesy of the Ohr-O'Keefe Museum of Art.

14: Photograph of downtown Biloxi, c. 1900, courtesy of the Ohr-O'Keefe Museum of Art.

15: George E. Ohr, c. 1900, courtesy of the Ohr-O'Keefe Museum of Art.

16: Drawing by William Woodward, George Ohr, and Joseph Meyer, New Orleans 1889. Snake jug, 1877, by Kirkpatrick, 11 in. (h), collection of Illinois State Museum.

17: Tchoutacabouffa River, courtesy of Land Trust for the Mississippi Coast Plain.

18: George E. Ohr's second pottery, c. 1894, courtesy of the Ohr-O'Keefe Museum of Art. Novelty assortment, c. 1895–96, inkwell with iguana-like creature; vase pinched into a face; log cabin; bird-in-hand inkwell; inkwell; pictograph coin. Collection of/photographed by Robert A. Ellison, Jr.

19: Bowl with folded alteration, c. 1897–1900, 3 ⅜ in. (h) x 6 15/16 (d), The Metropolitan Museum of Art, promised Gift of Robert A. Ellison Jr. (L.2009.22.281), photographed by Robert A. Ellison Jr. Vase (bottom), c. 1893–1909, 4 ⅜ in. (h) x 4 ½ in. (d), collection Kirkland Museum of Fine and Decorative Art, Denver.

20: Horticultural Hall, courtesy of Prints and Photographs, Library of Congress. Large urn, c. 1892, 62 in. (h), courtesy of the Ohr-O'Keefe Museum of Art.

21: Ewer, 1891, 13 in. (h), collection of/photographed by Robert A. Ellison, Jr.

22: Oil painting by William Woodward, George Ohr and Joseph Meyer, New Orleans, 1889, courtesy of the Ohr-O'Keefe Museum of Art.

23: Shoe group, c. 1888–1892, collection of/photographed by Robert A. Ellison, Jr.

24: The second pottery, 1894, courtesy of the Ohr-O'Keefe Museum of Art.

25: Tilted vase, c. 1897–1900, 9 ¼ in. (h) x 4 ½ in. (w), The Metropolitan Museum of Art, promised Gift of Robert A. Ellison Jr. (L.2009.22.257), photographed by Robert A. Ellison Jr.

26: Puzzle mug, c. 1900, 3 ½ in. (h) x 5 ⅛ in. (w) x 3 ⅝ in. (d), collection Kirkland Museum of Fine and Decorative Art, Denver. Clockface vase, c. 1898, 14 3/16 in. (h), The Metropolitan Museum of Art, promised gift of Robert A. Ellison Jr. (L.2009.22.304), photographed by Robert A. Ellison Jr.

27: Teapot, c. 1900–1909, 4 ¾ in. (h), collection of David and Jacqueline Charak. Wrinkled vase, c. 1897–1900, 3 ⅜ in. (h), collection of/photographed by Robert A. Ellison, Jr.; Trick photograph, courtesy of the author.

28: Four low pots, c. 1895–1900, 2 ⅛–2 ⅞ in. (h); mark detail, c. 1895–96, collection of/photographed by Robert A. Ellison, Jr.

29: Burnt bottle, 3 in. (h) x 2 ½ in (d), and cabinet vase, 4 ⅝ in. (h) x 3 ¼ in. (d), pre-1833 fire, collection Kirkland Museum of Fine and Decorative Art, Denver.

30: Day after fire, courtesy of the Ohr-O'Keefe Museum of Art.

31: Five red vases, c. 1895-1910, 3 ⅛–4 in. (h), collection of/photographed by Robert A. Ellison, Jr. Photograph of Ohr family, courtesy of the Ohr-O'Keefe Museum of Art.

32: Rebuilt studio with shoo-fly, c. 1895, George at International Exposition in Atlanta, 1895. Courtesy of the Ohr-O'Keefe Museum of Art.

33: Pottery showroom, 1898, courtesy of Prints and Photographs, Library of Congress.

34: Wide double-necked form, c. 1897–1900, 6 ⅜ in. (h) x 6 ¼ in. (w), collection of/photographed by Robert A. Ellison, Jr.

35: Ducktail pitcher, c. 1898–1910, 4 ⅝ in. (h) x 8 7/16 in (w), collection of/photographed by Robert A. Ellison, Jr.

36: Petticoat vase (left), c. 1899, 7 ¾ in. (h) x 4 ¾ in. (w); Vase (right), c. 1899, 6 ¼ in. (h) x 5 ¼ in. (w). Courtesy of the Ohr-O'Keefe Museum of Art. Red vase with black speckles (center), c. 1895–96, 7 9/16 in. (h), collection of/photographed by Robert A. Ellison, Jr.

37: Vase with double-looped handles (top left), c. 1899, 6 ½ in. (w), courtesy of the Ohr-O'Keefe Museum of Art. Dark crinkled pot (top right), c. 1897–1900, 6 ⅜ in. (h) x 6 in. (w); Two wide pots, c. 1898–1910, (left) 2 ¾ in. (h) x 7 ⅛ in. (w), (right) 4 ⅛ in. (h) x 7 in. (w). Collection of/photographed by Robert A. Ellison, Jr.

38: Scalloped form, c. 1897–1900, 3 ½ in. (h) x 6 in. (w), collection of/photographed by Robert A. Ellison, Jr.

39: Pitcher with snake handle, c. 1895–96, 8 ⅛ in. (h), collection of/photographed by Robert A. Ellison, Jr. George E. Ohr, courtesy of the Ohr-O'Keefe Museum of Art.

40: Two vases, (left) c. 1897–1900, 7 ½ in. (h), (right) c. 1895–96, 7 9/16 in (h); Totem-like form, c. 1897–1900, 7 1/16 in. (h). Collection of/photographed by Robert A. Ellison, Jr.

41: George in St. Louis with his prize-winning pots, 1904, courtesy of the Ohr-O'Keefe Museum of Art.

42: Pink ewer (top), c. 1897–1900, 8 ⅞ in. (h); Two striped bisque vessels, c. 1898–1910, (left) 4 in. (h) x 6 in. (w), (right) 5 in. (h) x 6 ⅞ in. (w). Collection of/photographed by Robert A. Ellison, Jr.

43: George in retirement, courtesy of the Ohr-O'Keefe Museum of Art.

44: George E. Ohr and sons in front of the remodeled pottery, around 1912, courtesy of the Ohr-O'Keefe Museum of Art.

45: Betty Woodman, twisted handle pillow pitcher (left), 1983, glazed earthenware, 20 in. (h), private collection, reproduced with permission from the artist. Richard Devore, Untitled (right), c. 1987–88, ceramic 15 ¾ in. (h) x 11 ½ in. (w), private collection, reproduced with permission of the Richard Devore Estate.

46: Biloxi Lighthouse pot, c. 1895, courtesy of the Ohr-O'Keefe Museum of Art.

47: Ohr-O'Keefe Museum, designed by Frank O. Gehry, courtesy of the Ohr-O'Keefe Museum of Art.

48: Shoo-fly of Ohr-O'Keefe Museum; Pleasant Reed Interpretive Center. Courtesy of the Ohr-O'Keefe Museum of Art.

49: Quintessential teapot, c. 1897–1900, 7 ¾ in. (h) x 7 ⅛ in. (w), The Metropolitan Museum of Art, promised gift of Robert A. Ellison Jr. (L.2009.22.278a,b), photographed by Robert A. Ellison Jr.

50: George E. Ohr, c. 1895 , courtesy of the Ohr-O'Keefe Museum of Art. Hands on Wheel, Mikhail Olykainen/ Shutterstock.com.

51: Red ewer, two tiered handle (top), c. 1897–1900, 9 ⅛ in. (h); Mud-dauber bisque vase (bottom left), c. 1898–1910, 8 ⅛ in. (h) x 8 in. (w); low pot (bottom right), c. 1895–1900, 2 ⅛–2 ⅞ in. (h). Collection of/photographed by Robert A. Ellison, Jr.

52: Vase, c. 1898–1910, 7 9/16 in. (h), collection of/ photographed by Robert A. Ellison, Jr.; Puzzle mug, c. 1900, 3 ⅝ in. (h) x 5 in. (w), courtesy of the Ohr-O'Keefe Museum of Art.

53: Vase with in-body-twist, c. 1900, 6 in. (h) x 3 ¼ in. (w), courtesy of the Ohr-O'Keefe Museum of Art.

Endpapers: George and one of his sons in pottery, c. 1905.